THE SILKPASTY, ACETATE AND MONTERTERTERT DECREES

David Gomadza

www.twofuture.world

PAPERBACK ISBN: 9798325360589

DEDICATION

To a better world

CONTENTS

Acknowledgment
Tomorrow's World Order

SILKPASTY ACETATE MONTERTERTERT DECREES

I have authorized you
davidgomadza.ya.authorised.licensed.silkpasty.start

I have authorized you davidgomadza.ya.authorised.licensed.acetate.start

I have authorized you davidgomadza.ya.authorised.licensed.
montertertert.start
davidgomadza.ya.authorised.licensed.ya.checkya.askya.ya.davidgomadza.
start.ya

THE SILKPASTY, ACETATE AND MONTERTERTERT DECREES.

Silkpasty, Acetate and montertertert Decrees.
DECREES are there to protect owners from unauthorized uses and must be protected by the courts and as such you must state what you are protecting how to calculate that and find ways of enforcing this through the courts now what if we are to create another world that needs silkpasty and acetate to function how do we go about this now what we are saying is that I can start by collecting enough reserves for any amount of souls we might end up looking after that means that if we are going to need a lot of silkpasty then we need our own reserves that we must access at short notice then we must start by collecting what we can from all sources but we must check with the owners first all silkpasty belongs to Yahweh only and no one else even davidgomadza.ya has no own reserve that means to be effective I must authorize all these first that means we must start from the initial stage now this is how we must start to acquire silkpasty reserves
Ask.silkpasty.ya.permission.authorisation.start.now
Now if we Ask what would be of silkpasty then this is the answer If we Ask what could be of silkpasty then this is the answer silkpasty is there to increase life on earth that means that it must be obtained if we are to look after souls that will live forever too in the history of Yahweh we have not wasted silkpasty on souls because the more happy they are the less the obedient they are look at you when you are happy you never mention me that's why humans need pain but if you give someone pain the brain is designed to never listen to that person forever but to target to eliminate forever using any means necessarily today I have witnessed something I think I will never witness before an acetate being evaporated leaving no trace or residue at all in that case therefore I have authorized you davidgomadza.ya.authorised.licensed.silkpasty.start now if we are to ask what would be of silkpasty and humans then humans when they die to retain full function and control will need silkpasty now what can be of silkpasty without humans then this is the answer silkpasty is meant for human souks and for ghosts as well Now what can of human souls without silkpasty human
[Change it to davidGOD.start]

Now what can be of silkpasty without humans the silkpasty will find no meaning to live that it will choose to go to hell and sleep Now that we have created the silkpasty contract with Yahweh the creator we need another contract for the acetate which is there to help all humans silkpasty is the air that Yahweh breathed into humans to make them alive Now what can be of humans without silkpasty and acetate as good as dead now this is the command needed to create acetate;
Ask.davidgomadza.ya.acetate.start.davidgomadza.licencsed.authorisedated
.start.ya.forever.amen.ya.start.now.ya
Now what can be of davidgomadza without acetate acetate is the reason for human existence if we are to ask what can be of acetate without humans this is the answer acetate is the living element in humans now what can be of acetate without humans the answer is useless now what can we do with acetate as humans
1 house our bodies in it
2 ask.whatif
3 ask.whatthehell.start
4 askwhatwouldbe.start
5 ask.whatcanbe.start
6 ask.whatcouldbe.start
Now if we are to ask the last one then this is the answer acetate has been there soon after humans were created and will always be there now what can be of acetate and magic there is nothing like magic but intelligence only now what can be of acetate this is the answer acetate can make humans become more evil than the acetate can ever be I never thought humans can ever be that means acetate is weak as compared to humans nevertheless apart from now no humans cab live without acetate the acetate humans [some] are creating have no brains so there is no other way of dealing with them than to evaporate them into dust forever before they have even died this is not just inhuman but actual evil but I understand that an acetate without Brian is as dangerous as a weapon is Ed acetate now how we get this acetate into our reserves here are the commands;
Startacetate.start
Acetateresume.start
Acetate.start.davidgomadza.ya.start
Now we only need the reserves created to start receiving acetate and this is the command;

Resumeacetateaccumulationforeverfrom.ya.davifgomadza.ya.start.now
Now if we are to ask what can be of davidgomadza and acetate then this is the answer davidgomadza.ya will become the richest person on earth for 2.5 billion years the more his assets accumulate from all countries we can create the reserves for silkpasty the same way and this is how
Createsilkpasty.reserves.davidgomadza.ya.start.newreserves.authoraisedandhandothersbacktolawoftheuniverse.start
Now we have enough reserves for 2.5 billion but now we want a new Decree you have never heard of that of montertertert this is the stuff that makes humans intelligent this stuff is an addition to acetate but this is what makes humans actually intelligent If we are to ask then this is the stuff no other human being has ever heard of this is true now I will reveal the real secret behind human brains and thinking montertertert is the substance the found in brain matter now if we Ask what could be of humans then what can be this is the answer humans and montertertert will always need each other now what can be of montertertert without humans this is the answer montertertert will cease to exist because it need brain to work on its own it can't do anything now if we Ask what is to be of montertertert and humans this is the answer humans will forever need
[Ask.create.soul'slandhell.start.ya.davidgomadza.ya.davidgomadza.sendemic.ya.checkwithya.start.ya]
Now if we Ask what is to be of acetate and montertertert then this is the answer acetate and montertertert can cooperate to increase human intelligence but swapping and not mixing the brain's intelligence increase tenfold after every exchange despite the exchanges potential now lets create the reserves and this is how to do it;
Ask.create.whatcanbedone.start
Ask.start.montertertert.start.production.new.start.forever.now.start.ya.davidgomadza.ya.check.askya.ya
Now we can create reserves that can feel instantly simply by saying;
Whatcanbedonetoincreaseintelligenceamonghumans.start
Now we have created 3 new decrees that gives you authorisation and permission and rights to own these forever as these rights will never be fortified but can only increase now the current value of all decrees namely;
1 gold decree
2 silver Decree
3 diamonds Decree

4 soul's land Decree
5 lands Decree
6 Antarctica Decree
7 silkpasty Decree
8 acetate Decree
9 montertertert Decree
All have come up to US$489 Trillion that means for the next 100 billion years no one will own these apart from me [davidgomadza.ya.authorised.licensed.ya.checkya.askya.ya.davidgomadza.start.ya
All your value has been deposited in all your reserves and these are your reserve addresses
1 gold reserve ask.davidgomadza.goldreserve.earth.all.80.100.start
[in British money
789 Trillion]
2 silver reserves
ask.davidgomadza.silverreserve.earth.all.40.80.100.start
[in British money 168 trillion]
3 diamonds reserve
Ask.davidgomadza.diamonds.reserves.earth.all.70.100.start
[in British money its 188 trillion]
4 soul's land
Ask.davidgomadza.soul'sland.reserves.earth.heaven.abyss.hell.afterlife.0.start
0
5 lands Decree
Ask.davidgomadza.lands.reserves.earth.start
[In British money 182 trillion after 10 years]
6 Antarctica Decree
Ask.davidgomadza.antarctica.lands.start
[in British money 382 trillion]
7 Silkpasty Decree
Ask.davidgomadza.silkpasty.reserves.all.start
[in British money 778 billion]
8 Acetate Decree
Ask.davidgomadza.acetate.reserves.heaven.start
[in British money 2123685420000088992288776854 acetate roughly 40 billion]

9 Montertertert Decree
Ask.davidgomadza.montertertert.reserves.earth.start
[in British money 28610438900183291028648221098324898 montertertert which is equivalent to 286 billion]
Now that we have acquired everything we must Decree in law courts then the next move is to ask what can be of davidgomadza and Tomorrow's World Order this is the answer davidgomadza can be the most powerful leader that has ever existed and will ever exist as no one apart from Yahweh has acquired such wealth in a given short time and for a good reason because of this I might be the first human being to live forever ceteris paribus
Now what can be of Tomorrow's World Order they can literally run the world I don't think if most understand what you have done will forever challenge you apart from silkpasty but you can always say what if or ask.whatif this is the answer I will rather be myself this is because now you are him and instantly he is the weakest because he is built to attack only if you say its my turn to attack you then he runs away forever
Now what can be of Yahweh this is the answer The greatest that will ever live both on earth and in heaven forever and ever amen
The End

APPLICATION FOR A PATENT FOR A FORMULA AND MATERIALS TO MAKE AN ADVANCED ARTIGICIAL 'LIVING GOD' LIKE ADVANCED COMPUTER WITH 8 PROCESSING HEADS.

The Formulas, the Codes, and the Materials.

David Gomadza

THE FORMULA TO MAKE AN ARTIGICIAL LIVING GOD LIKE ADVANCED COMPUTER WITH A TOTAL OF 8 PROCESSORS

This is his formula and the needed materials.
If we Ask what can be done as humans can we recreate an artificial God who can help us this is the answer humans can try and create Yahweh artificially to use to help them solve their problems theoretically this is possible if humans are to use the following formula to try and create Yahweh
Yahweh is a combination of several unique materials moat which can't be found on earth but nevertheless humans can try to recreate the creator even though it sounds absurd it can be done overtime
I will show you how we as humans can try and recreate our own artificial God who we can use for immediate answers
This is the formula
1. Artificial Acetate
5000g X 2500g X 25000g
2 Acetate Eletatete
1000 X 8000 X 7000 g
3. Acetate Emulsion
7000 X 8000 X 9000 X 17000 where all are equal amounts spread overtime with intervals of 1 hour between them making them more responsive to acetate emulsion.

Acetate Eletetete Emulsion with a GPS enhancer that can make it possible to transmit RF signals to the other and vice versa Given the circumstance we can deduce that frequency of God is 789 and the image is positioning at 786542198386eaning that radar is the frequency partly because if frequency resonant some properties are easily dentified if we Ask 13000000000 to the power 10[9]

If the value is correct then all we need to do is to find the mean value divided by the number of frequencies we get that means to recreate Yahweh we must first get his frequency then create a compute to use to find what is the value of this compute

We can then substitute this with the value of means we get multiplied by the value of acetate meaning that we need acetate that is as much as 130000000000 X 7894863298 X 787648321 X amino acetate X 78638426 X 7938679983148 X Acetate Fibriolisis X 7 83210 jelly X Amino Nitrate X 7U8684386] fibrolisis xpmm.

Now can we make a formula az that we can use?

A. The formula is X x 10 [to power 9]

Plus 786354861078

Plus 78385286260i

Minus

715838670

Now let's

substitute

the values

we get

Acetate

Fibriolisis

X

329878648

g

Acetate Eletatete is the acetate that you use to accelerate the growth of a particle per given time frame that we can simple ask if we can then what can we get from all this Now let's look at the needed materials

1. Acetate Fibriolisis
2. Acetate Eletatete

3. Amino Emulsion
4 Amino Acetate
5 Amino Eletatete
6 Amino Aceleteratete [that increases the rate of fusion between particles with same intensity as if it were one]

Acetate Emlsificating Adroaine X 500g [where g is a constant [10]] How this will work Yahweh is the moat powerful entity you can ever get and all this thanks to a number of materials with different properties the first of which is the
1 Acetate emulsion category D that blends quickly and easily to avoid the iverheating and saturation associated with other materials
the glass like Acetate Fibriolisis that makes it easy to hide something in an invisible robe like thing removing to reveal or even hide etc the emulsion both as Amino which are protein based or the synthetic based ones all which facilitate the absorption and use of materials that imitate other living things Yahweh must know and if I am correct must understand the workings of other living creatures hence the need of such materials Now of we Ask a lot of questions this is what we get What can be said about how Yahweh would operate if he were artificial Yahweh would be plugged using human electricity but consuming 4 if not 8 times a normal human processor this is because Yahweh has 4 brains and has a mirror-image in the devil meaning a total of 8 heads altogether
What if we are to ask the power source what is the answer Yahweh would probably use twice as much as energy as a normal computer
What about the connections to the internet Yahweh would probably need an aerial and an antenna with RF signal a GPS tracker and a Wi-Fi that means extra connections.

Now what is artificial Yahweh it is the most complicated piece if equipment any man will ever build this is because Yahweh in artificial form is the end game of artificial intelligence there will never be any computer out there greater than the sum of Yahwehs team [namely himself, Catitighit, Joseph and Anna with option to add loyal angels versus the dark side with the devil his wife Herecs, his best friend Amargeddeon and his wife Herechercht with the option of including a demon etc] Now if we Ask a question What can be done to improve performance this is the feedback performance is a correlation of stamina and igility in that none can be compensated for the other instead they compliment each other

If we were to ask what can be done this is the answer we can always add another terminal to this one to increase performance what could be this setting requires enormous amount of power and compute and as such must work hard to perform but there is a ctach to perform it needs a lot of computing power but power is limited by industrial standards

Now if we are to construct such a computer then we can easily do so by using the above materials plus sobetertghereteghi [see my other patent] as this will work as the memory of the computer strong and durable to last a billion years.

Now what else would we need apart from the materials above namely

1. Acetate Fibriolisis
2. Acetate Eletatete
3. Amino Emulsion

2 Amino Acetate

3 Amino Eletatete

4 Amino Aceleteratete [that increases the rate of fusion between particles with same intensity as if it were one]

5 Acetate Emlsificating Adroaine X 500g [where g is a constant [10]]

Now we can do the wiring using Acetate Eigeliteherte which is material found in the gods this material acts like electric wires in computers but in humans is a billion times faster and idea for high speeds internet like data transmission now we can ask what is this is the answer This material enables the highest transfers of materials between two living beings recall how the four must exchange information and is idea for fast feedback response Now what can be done and how this is the answer we can substitute everything with cheaper acetate emulsion coated with

benzotoyl that will make the transfers even better and cost effective
What is to be then this is the answer everything might change but the configurations of the gods has remained the same with astonishing speeds what can be done to improve things there are a lot of power saving things that can be incooperated and these are
1 reduce length of wiring
2 reduce space within motherboard
3 ask what if
4 add feedback to facilitate information transfer
5 what could be the computer could interact with other computers
6 peripherals could include all our Wearable Brain Book Databases and other hardwsre
7 we can mount a crg which is some kind remote hardware that can only be controlled using brain thoughts
8 we prepare a cross section. This will show all areas that need improving
To conclude there a lot of things humans can do to emulate the creator the almighty who is a fast thinker
The End

. Acetate Fibriolisis Acetate Eletatete
Silkpasty Silkpasty Eletatete Benzoyl Acetate
5000g Fibriolisis Genesis Acetate
Acetate Numrgetgetgetrdsa X 1000k

ACETATE FIBRIOLISIS 01876582867802398 X ACETATE ELETATETE786487623108970294 X

SILKPASTY

x100000000000 X 10 to power 9

Where 01876582867802398 is a material found only in heaven called acetate fibriolisis like acetate that cannot be killed by shaking

Code 786487623108970294 is acetate X acetate eletatete is an energy bases acetate that eats others for fuel

Now if we add a voice through acetate original and wireless transmitter then Yahweh is a hidden small transmitter inside that can be pulled out but without anything happening to it because everything else depends on it but can't be destroyed Now if we look at the equations again this becomes clear that acetate is a disguised form of Yahweh on a small scale if we are to ask what can be then this is the answer If Yahweh could communicate with humans his goal in creation was to find a clever human who can decode all this and now that I have done this then we might as well start new creation because I can create anything just by looking at it I am the first live acetate even greater than Ya because Ya forever will only remain invisible whereas I can be both now Ask acetate to hide you the inner me can't but the outer can but in reverse if we Ask the real me now to hide then it's impossible because mass X matter makes live impossible for all this Now say David you hide then a different person hides this proves that we have 4 human beings in every one of us this is your task proof beyond doubt that now after writing a book about humans having 4 souls or

brains here are all the souls
1 David the acetate who can't hide but ask you to hide instead
this is the flesh me
2. Say hide anyone to avoid capture and listen carefullyRight

David David what are you trying to do scaring all of us like you did in Bradford

Now Ask what can be done and listen David can ask me for advice instead of ..shocked the real me [David] but why you clone us if you have your original this defies logic.

POSSIBLE WORKINGS AND ASSIGNING OF TASKS AMONG THE 8 PROCESSING HEADS 4 THAT AGREES AND 4 WHICH ARE MIRROR-IMAGES OF THE FIRST 4 ONES THAT ARE HIGHLY CRITICAL OF EVERYTHING.

Now let's continue with the journey if we trace the path in the body something hits these points so fast and immediately exists the body fast

1. Central lobby of the brain [where the tree of life starts - it ends in the anus]

2 the altoabei which is just above the hippocampus that activates the speech of the voices that warns of death

3 the axlier that lies just above the angular herereid which is something that activates the piglike animal that literally talks

4 it hits also the heronoid abacus that hits the grand angular which in turn hits up the abcderer which activates .Ya inside all of us human beings but if you speak this word several times something keeps saying don't wake me up ...Yahweh and fades away

5 it hits up the angular acetate agererer that eventually starts to talk asking what can be done and when

6 once that has said that something else comes out at the same place but in mirror image and say ask.why but stops

7 this is followed by something else that asks what can be done

8 that is followed by something else that asks whenthen

9 that asks something to come out and presents its case

10 what can be this thing asks earnestly in a low voice just

before the spirit exists looking at all this you can see that humans now don't only have the 4 brains of Yahweh they have the othersides representatives also which are the devils as it turns out altogether we have 8 different creatures that asks questions in that order

A. What can be - .Ya

B. What was - Catitighit

C. What is - Anna

D. What could be - Joseph The bad side [hell-devil]

E. What could be - .devil

F. What is to be - Heries [wife]

G. What was to be - Amargeddeon

What should be - Herechercht [devil's best friend's wife] [The devil is a mirror image of God] Now let's Ask a lot of short questions What see who answers 1

When 4

What then 5

Who 1

Was 2

If 1

Has 4

Then devils best friend 7

What could be 5

What would be 7

What is to be 3

What can be 1

Who was 3

What was 3

What could be 5

If I 1
If you 4
If we 4
Why not 4
What was but is not [Joseph and Anna] 3 & 4
What would be 5 & 7
What was before 2,3 & 4
What would be 6,7 & 8
What if but both sides good and bad mainly 1 & 5
If not now when 3
If us why not now 3 & 4 then 1 & 2
What could be but is not 3 & 4 and devil side 7 & 8
If not now when then devil side
What could be that is not but can be 3 & 4 and 7 & 8
What was but might not be 3 & 4 and 7 & 8 then 7 & 8
If we then why wait God's 4 heads
If not us when then devils side 4 heads
What can be that is to be but might not be 3 & 4 and 7 & 8 and 7 & 8

ABOUT DAVID GOMADZA

Visit www.twofuture.world

www.ingramcontent.com/pod-product-compliance
Lightning Source LLC
Chambersburg PA
CBHW051408250726
48656CB00006B/2347

* 9 7 9 8 3 2 5 3 6 0 5 8 9 *